ORIGAMI ADVENTU...

DINOSAURS

First edition for the United States, its territories and dependencies, and Canada published in 2006 by Barron's Educational Series, Inc.

A Quarto Children's Book

Copyright © 2006 Quarto Children's Books Ltd.

All inquiries should be addressed to:
Barron's Educational Series, Inc.
250 Wireless Boulevard
Hauppauge, NY 11788
www.barronseduc.com

ISBN-13: 978-0-7641-5970-1
ISBN-10: 0-7641-5970-4

Library of Congress Control Number 2005934858

Design Tall Tree Ltd.
Author and origami model design Nick Robinson
The Pteranodon and Psittacosaurus were co-designed by Mark Leonard, and Nick Robinson,
the Velociraptor by Ron Nichols, the Plesiosaur by Mark Leonard,
and the Antarctosaurus by Samuel Randlett. All other designs by Nick Robinson.
Editor Christa Garidis
Art Director Jonathan Gilbert
Illustrations Sebastian Quigley and Nick Robinson
Consultant Paleontologist Dr. Sue Gay

Printed in China
9 8 7 6 5 4 3 2 1

ORIGAMI ADVENTURES

DINOSAURS

AND OTHER PREHISTORIC CREATURES

Nick Robinson

BARRON'S

Origami

Origami is the Japanese word for paper folding, and it dates back many hundreds of years. Today, it is a widespread creative art practiced by millions of people all around the world. The basics are simple, but it can take a lifetime to become an origami master.

Using this book

This book contains a collection of colorful models with easy-to-follow instructions and diagrams to help you complete each of them. Carefully read through the instructions before you start each model. At the back of the book are a few black and white practice sheets. Use these to perfect your techniques before starting on the finished models.

★ There is a small star at the start of each project and at certain important stages. As you make each model, make sure that this matches the position of the star on your model sheet so that the pattern on the finished dinosaur is in the correct position.

The Path to Success

Each of the models in this book is graded in terms of difficulty. Make sure that you start with the simplest models first and work your way through the book. That way you will learn all the techniques to become an origami master.

DIFFICULTY ★☆☆☆

Beginner
These simple models use just a couple of the easiest folding techniques.

DIFFICULTY ★★☆☆

Apprentice
New techniques are introduced, making these models a little more difficult.

DIFFICULTY ★★★☆

Expert
These models will start to use some of the more complicated origami techniques.

DIFFICULTY ★★★★

Master
By including all the techniques learned in the book, these models are only for origami experts.

Take a look at the "Tips and Tricks" section on page 48 before you start.

Techniques

Here are some of the techniques you will need to complete the models in this book. You should practice these with some scrap paper until you can complete them easily. Try altering the angles and distances to see how these affect the results. However complex the origami designs, they all use the techniques listed here.

Valley fold

Fold the paper away from you and use an index finger to make the crease.

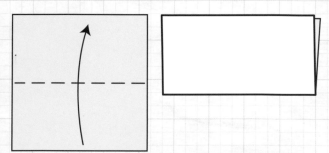

Mountain fold

This is the opposite of the valley fold. Fold the paper toward you.

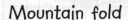

Vertical fold

Horizontal fold

Outside reverse fold

Both folded layers wrap around on opposite sides, to the outside of the paper beneath.

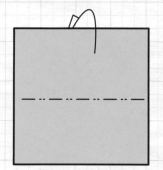

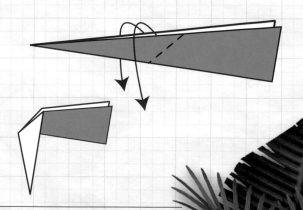

Inside reverse fold

The folded layers are pushed inside the original layers of paper.

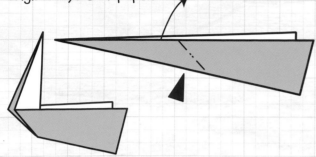

Double reverse fold

If you make an inside and then an outside reverse fold, you can create heads or beaks.

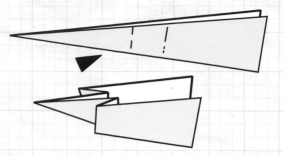

Inside crimp

Make valley and mountain folds on both sides, with the folded parts swivelling inside.

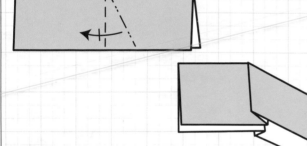

Outside crimp

A similar move, but the paper swivels on the outside, rather than the inside.

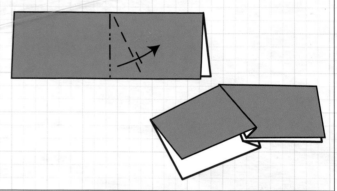

★ **Starting point star**
Use this to orient your sheet. It corresponds to the star mark on the model sheet.

 **Fold and unfold**
Shows that a fold is not permanent.

○ **Reference point circle**
Pay attention to this point.

Repeat
Repeat the last move you made. The number of lines that cross the arrow indicate how many times you should repeat the move.

 Turnover
Turn the whole model over.

— — — — — — **Mountain fold crease**
Shows where a mountain fold is made.

— — — — — **Valley fold crease**
Shows where a valley fold is made.

▼ **Pressure**
Push at this point and in this direction.

Pleat
Make a pleat fold at this point.

Curl
Curl this part of your model.

Open out
Open this part of the model.

Tyrannosaurus Rex

When it roamed the planet about 70 million years ago, Tyrannosaurus Rex was one of the largest meat-eating dinosaurs around. It could grow up to 49 ft (15 m) long, stand 20 ft (6 m) tall, and weigh a massive 6 tons (6,100 kg). It had an enormous head that many scientists believe supported powerful muscles. These could deliver tremendous force to the jaws, allowing the dinosaur to crunch its way through even the largest prey.

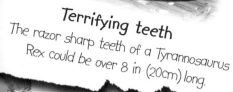

Terrifying teeth
The razor sharp teeth of a Tyrannosaurus Rex could be over 8 in (20cm) long.

FACT

Some scientists believe that Tyrannosaurus Rex survived by scavenging off the dead bodies of other dinosaurs.

Make a T. Rex

DIFFICULTY ★ ★ ★

Fold your very own ferocious T. Rex model.

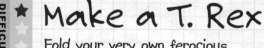

1 Start with the model sheet white side up. Valley fold along a diagonal, crease, and unfold. Valley fold the two outer corners into this crease.

2 Valley fold the upper edges to the center.

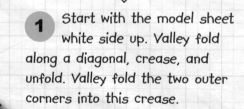

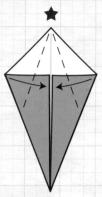

6

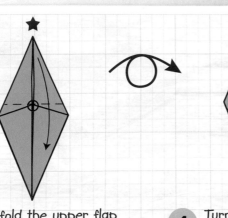

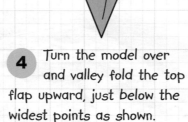

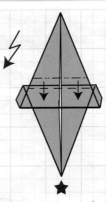

3 Valley fold the upper flap down at the point where the two corners folded in step 2 meet (as shown by the circle above).

4 Turn the model over and valley fold the top flap upward, just below the widest points as shown.

5 Make a pleat to the top triangular section as shown.

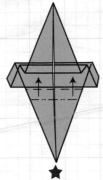

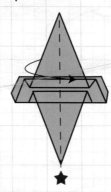

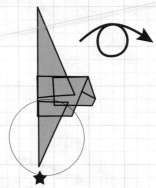

6 And another pleat to the lower triangular section.

7 Valley fold the whole model in half from left to right.

8 Now focus on the head. Turn the model over.

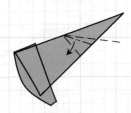

9 Make a crimp fold to lower the head.

This is how your finished T. Rex model should look.

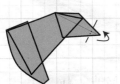

10 Mountain fold the tip of the head behind.

Dimetrodon

The most obvious feature of a Dimetrodon was the large fin on its back. This fin may have played an important role in controlling the animal's body temperature. As a cold-blooded animal, Dimetrodon would have had to warm its blood in the morning before it could hunt. The huge sail-like fin was full of blood vessels, which made this warm-up much faster than in other animals.

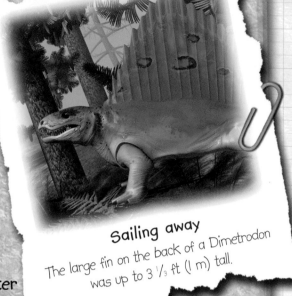

Sailing away
The large fin on the back of a Dimetrodon was up to 3 ⅓ ft (1 m) tall.

FACT
Dimetrodon was not actually a dinosaur. It belonged to a family called Pelycosaurs that roamed the earth about 40 million years before the dinosaurs.

DIFFICULTY ★★★

Make a Dimetrodon
You have two color model sheets so you can fold your own pair of Dimetrodons.

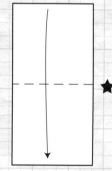

1 Start with the model sheet white side up. Valley fold the upper short edge to meet the lower short edge and crease.

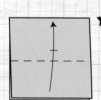

2 Valley fold a single lower edge to the top edge, and repeat on the other side.

8

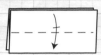

3 Once again, valley fold a single layer from the top to the bottom edge and repeat on the other side.

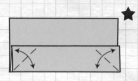

4 Valley fold the short edges over to lie along the lower edge, crease firmly, and unfold.

5 Carefully inside reverse fold the corners using the creases you have just made and repeat on the other side.

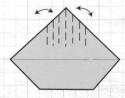

6 Swing the flap downward on both sides of the model.

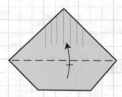

7 Valley fold the left and right-hand edges into the center to form the fin.

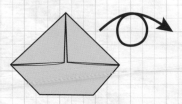

8 Like this. Turn the paper over.

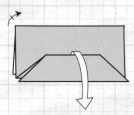

9 Add a series of mountain and valley creases to simulate the bones in the fin.

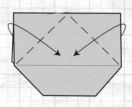

10 Valley fold the lower flaps back up on both sides.

11 Fold back the left top layer of the flap to the right to expose the face. Valley fold the right-hand flap over at an angle to form a leg. Repeat both steps on the other side.

12 Valley fold the left-hand flaps to match the right, forming the front legs.

This is how your finished Dimetrodon model should look.

Pteranodon

These flying reptiles used rising currents of warm air to lift themselves into the sky, just as a modern glider does. Scientists are not sure what the large crest on the back of the head was for. Some believe it was used to steer Pteranodon as it flew through the air, while others believe that it acted as a counterweight to keep the extremely long head balanced.

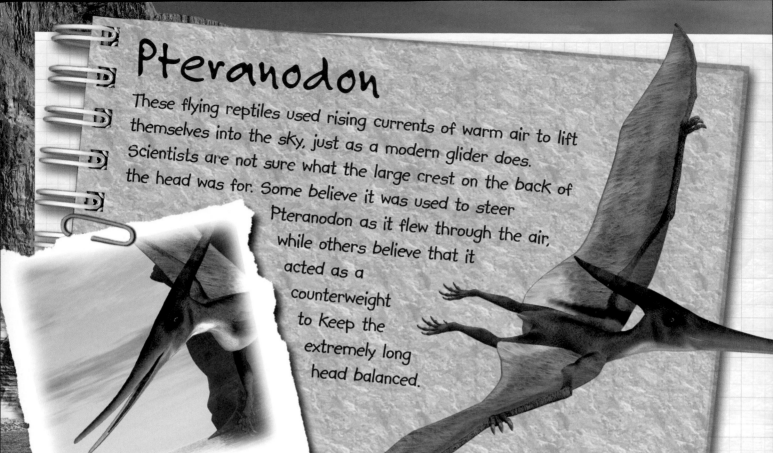

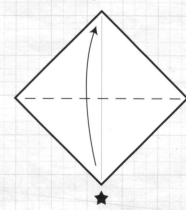

Toothless

Pteranodons had no teeth in their long mouths. They scooped fish up and swallowed them whole.

FACT

Pteranodons had an enormous wingspan, measuring up to 30 ft (9 m) from wingtip to wingtip—that is, nearly the length of five adults lying end to end!

DIFFICULTY ★ ★ ★ ★

Make a Pteranodon

Make this simple model of a flying reptile.

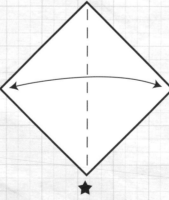

★

1 Start with the model sheet white side up. Valley fold along a diagonal, crease, and unfold.

★

2 Valley fold the lower corner up to meet the upper corner.

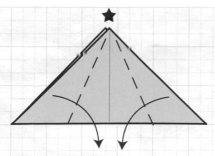

3 Valley fold the outer edges in and downward to meet the vertical center crease.

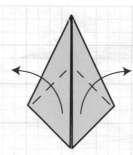

4 Valley fold the bottom corners back out so that the upper edges formed are horizontal.

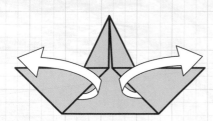

5 Open out the folds made in steps 3 and 4.

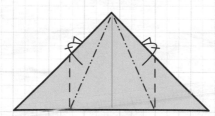

6 Using the folds made in steps 3 and 4, make inside crimp folds on both sides of the model to shape the wings.

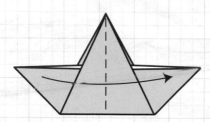

7 Valley fold the model in half from left to right.

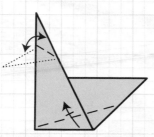

8 Valley fold the top corner over to form a head. Crease and unfold. Valley fold the lower corners in to shape the wings on both sides.

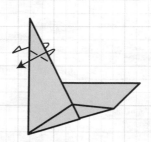

9 Make an outside reverse fold to bring the head forward.

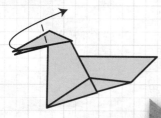

10 Make another reverse fold on the top layer of the head, to form the crest.

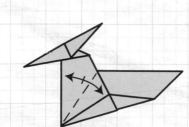

11 Add a valley crease on both sides to shape the wings.

This is how your finished Pteranodon model should look.

11

Stegosaurus

Even though the Stegosaurus measured up to 33 ft (10 m) long and weighed over 2 tons (2.030 kg), it was a plant eater and posed little threat to other dinosaurs—unless they wanted to eat one! Then these peaceful creatures turned into heavily armored fighting machines, complete with a row of bristling armor plates along their backs. These plates measuring up to 30 in (75 cm) long were bony-covered scales like those on the backs of crocodiles today.

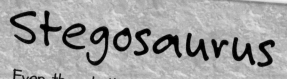

Prehistoric club
The large spikes on the end of the tail were used to defend Stegosaurus from attack.

FACT
Despite its large size, Stegosaurus had a brain only the size of a walnut.

DIFFICULTY ★★★★★

Make a Stegosaurus
You have two color model sheets to make a pair of dinosaurs.

 ★

1 Start with the model sheet white side up and valley fold in half.

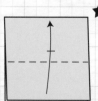 ★

2 Valley fold the top flap up to the upper edge. Repeat on the other side.

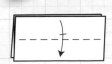

3 Valley fold this flap back down again. Repeat on the other side.

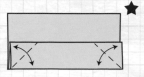

4 Valley fold the short edges over to lie along the lower edge, crease firmly, and unfold.

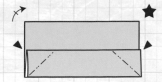

5 Using the creases made in step 4, make inside reverse folds on these corners. Repeat steps 4 and 5 on the other side.

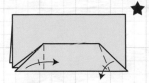

6 Open the top layer of the left side to the right as shown. Valley fold the right flap down to form a leg. Repeat on the other side.

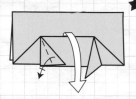

7 Valley fold the left flap down to form a leg, repeating on the other side. Now unfold the large flap downward.

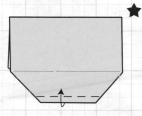

8 Valley fold over a small strip. Repeat steps 7 and 8 on the other side.

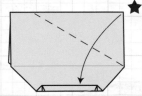

9 Starting at the lower-right corner, valley fold the top right corner over so that it touches the inside lower edge.

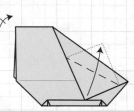

10 Valley fold the point partly out to meet the dotted line as shown. Repeat the last two steps on the other side.

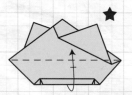

11 Valley fold the lower flaps up on either side.

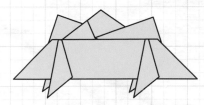

12 Open out the bottom of the model slightly so that it stands on its own.

This is how your finished Stegosaurus model should look.

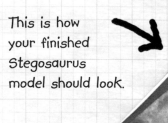

Psittacosaurus

This dinosaur lived in what is now China and Mongolia. It grew to about 8 ft (2.5 m) in length and had a long tail that it used to balance itself when walking or running on its hind legs. At the back of this dinosaur's head was a thick ridge of bone. This made Psittacosaurus' head square-shaped and acted as a fixing point for the strong muscles that operated the powerful, beaklike jaws.

Plant eater

Psittacosaurus probably used its toothless, beaklike jaws to pick off fruits and nuts.

DIFFICULTY ★ ★

Make a Psittacosaurus

Try out this simple model of a Psittacosaurus.

★

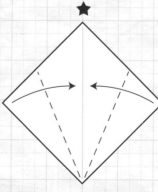

1 Start with model sheet white side up. Valley fold along a diagonal, crease, and unfold. Valley fold both lower edges to meet this crease.

14

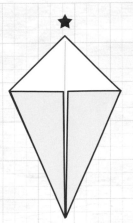

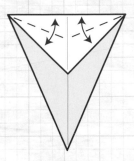

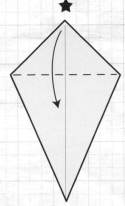

2 Turn the paper over.

3 Valley fold the triangular flap down at the top.

4 Valley fold each lower edge up to the top edge but only crease up to the center fold as shown.

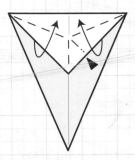

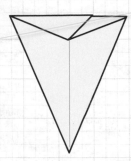

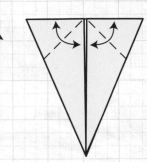

5 Valley fold both creases together, pinching the paper into a point, which you flatten to the right.

6 At this stage your model should look like this.

7 Turn the model over and valley fold each half of the upper edge to the vertical center. Crease and unfold.

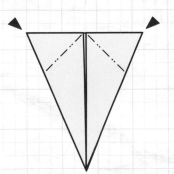

8 Using the creases made in step 7, inside reverse both these corners.

FACT

Psittacosaurus means "parrot lizard" and refers to the beaklike jaws of this dinosaur.

15

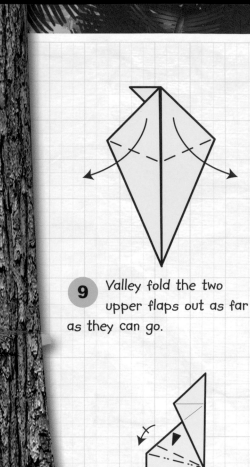

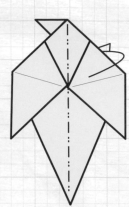

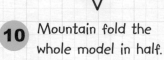

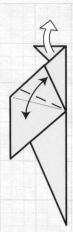

9 Valley fold the two upper flaps out as far as they can go.

10 Mountain fold the whole model in half.

11 Carefully unfold the head section. Make a crease at a slight angle to the existing crease, then unfold. Repeat on the other side.

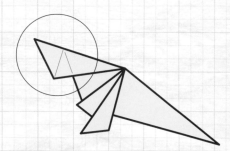

12 Make a crimp on both sides using the creases shown.

13 Valley fold the flap over to form a leg. Repeat on the other side.

14 Now focus on the head.

FACT

Psittacosaurus lived during the Early Cretaceous period, which was about 125 million years ago.

15 Mountain fold the tip of the head behind.

16 Make an inside reverse fold as shown.

17 Tuck the flap inside to "lock" the head together.

FACT

Psittacosaurus could walk on two or four legs, but would have run on its two hind legs to escape predators.

This is how your finished Psittacosaurus model should look.

Styracosaurus

Styracosaurus lived about 70 million years ago and measured up to 17 ft (5 m) long. It was an extremely well-armored dinosaur with a great number of sharp horns around its head. These horns protected the neck of Styracosaurus and were very useful when attacking the soft underbelly of a predator, such as Tyrannosaurus. If threatened by an approaching predator, Styracosaurus probably lowered its head and charged the meat eater head on, just like a modern-day rhino.

Charge!
Styracosaurus had a ring of horns around the frill and a large horn on its nose.

DIFFICULTY

Make a Styracosaurus
Practice your pleats before starting this model.

FACT
Styracosaurus had teeth in its cheeks and used these to chew its food. Other dinosaurs had to swallow their food whole.

1 Start with the model sheet colored side up. Valley fold along a diagonal, crease, and unfold. Valley fold in half but only pinch at the center, as shown, and unfold.

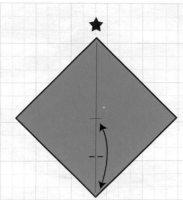

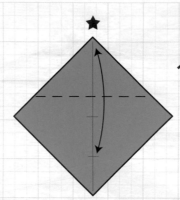

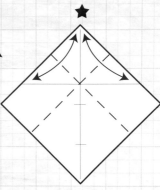

2 Valley fold the lower corner to this pinch, make another gentle pinch, and unfold.

3 Valley fold the upper corner to the pinch made in step 2, crease, and unfold.

4 Turn the sheet over and valley fold the top corner to meet one end of the crease made in step 3. Unfold and repeat on the other side.

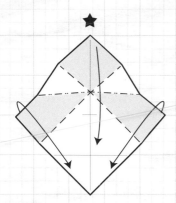

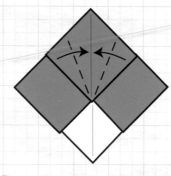

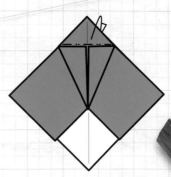

5 Using the creases made in steps 3 and 4, bring the upper three corners down to collapse the paper.

6 Valley fold the lower edges of the small square to the vertical center as shown.

7 Mountain fold the upper triangular flap behind.

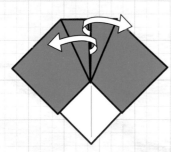

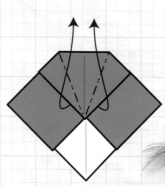

8 Open out the two flaps folded in step 6.

9 Lift the top layer of the lower corner of the square, opening it upward, and carefully flatten into a diamond shape.

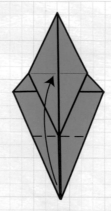

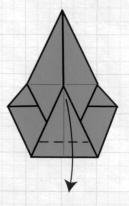

10 Valley fold the lower edges to the vertical center, tucking them under the upper diamond.

11 Valley fold the lower corner to the center of the diamond.

12 Leave a small gap, then valley fold the flap down again.

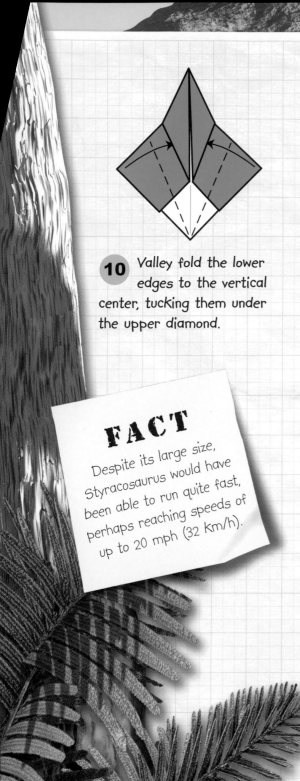

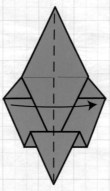

13 Valley fold the model in half from left to right.

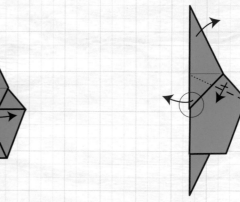

14 Hold the body section, then carefully ease the tip indicated by the circle away from the rest of the model. A new crease forms, pointing to the corner. When in position, flatten the paper so that it stays in place.

15 Ease open the head from behind. The eye indicates the angle you should look at to see the next step.

16 Valley fold the lower corner of the kite shape to the upper corner.

17 Make two valley folds at a slight angle and press the tip of the point together as you valley fold the body in half again. This will form a point.

18 Narrow the chin area by making mountain folds to each side and make gentle mountain creases to suggest legs.

FACT

Scientists have found large numbers of Styracosaurus bones together, indicating that they lived in large herds.

This is how your finished Styracosaurus model should look.

Spinosaurus

This enormous dinosaur was one of the largest carnivores (meat eaters) on the planet. It measured up to 60 ft (20 m) long and weighed up to 6 tons (6,100 kg) —that is, about the same weight as a Tyrannosaurus Rex. Its most obvious feature was an enormous fin on its back, which may have helped to regulate the dinosaur's body temperature in the same way as the fin on a Dimetrodon. This terrifying dinosaur probably fed on reptiles such as turtles.

Gone fishing
The claws on Spinosaurus' hands were elongated, making them ideal for hooking fish.

DIFFICULTY ★★☆☆

Make a Spinosaurus
Practice your reverse folds before starting this model.

1 Start with the model sheet colored side up. Valley fold both diagonals, crease, and unfold.

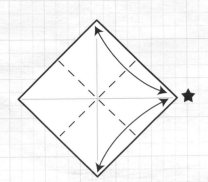

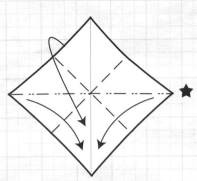

2 Turn the paper over, valley fold the opposite edges together, as shown, crease, and unfold.

3 Using the creases already formed, fold the outer corners down to the bottom corner and flatten the upper quarter on top.

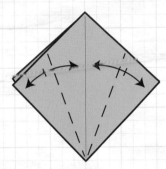

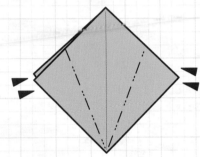

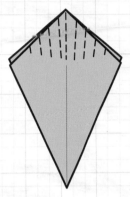

4 Valley fold the lower edges to the vertical center, crease, and unfold. Repeat on the other side.

5 Inside reverse the four flaps, both front and back, to create a Kite shape.

6 Make creases as shown to represent the "spines."

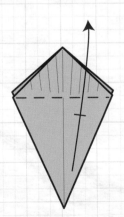

7 Valley fold the lower point upward and repeat on the other side.

FACT

The enormous sail on the back of Spinosaurus was up to 6 ft (2 m) tall—that is, as tall as an adult human!

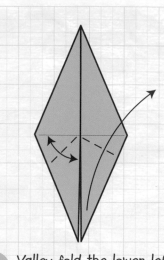

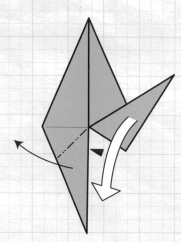

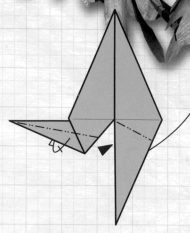

8 Valley fold the lower-left flap over so that the edge is horizontal. Crease and unfold. Valley fold the lower-right flap over at a shallower angle.

9 Inside reverse fold the lower-left flap to form the tail section. Unfold the flap on the right back to the vertical.

10 Using the crease made in steps 8 and 9, inside reverse fold the lower-right flap. Narrow the tail section with mountain folds on both sides.

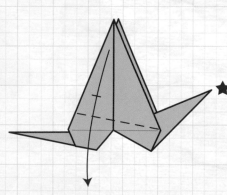

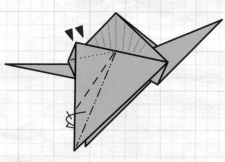

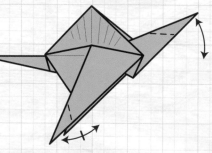

11 Valley fold the leg flaps down at a slight angle on both sides.

12 Look at the diagram carefully. The idea is to swivel paper behind the leg to form the foot. A new crease is formed where the dotted line is. Repeat on the other leg.

13 Valley fold the head and feet, crease, and unfold.

FACT

Some scientists believe that a male Spinosaurus used its sail to threaten other males or to attract females.

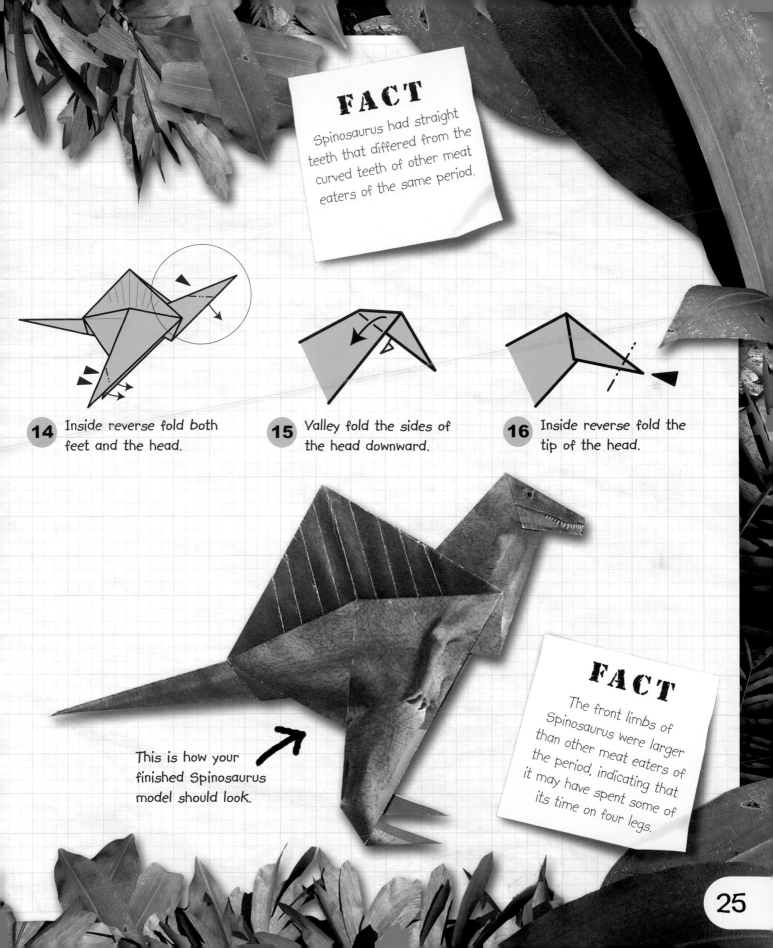

14 Inside reverse fold both feet and the head.

15 Valley fold the sides of the head downward.

16 Inside reverse fold the tip of the head.

This is how your finished Spinosaurus model should look.

Dinosaur Hatchling

Just like modern reptiles, dinosaurs laid eggs. Some simply buried their eggs and left the newly hatched young to fend for themselves. Others, however, looked after their young, building special nests for the eggs and watching over the young dinosaurs. Remains of one species of dinosaur, Maiasaura, have been found in large groups, with adults and young together, indicating that they took great care of their offspring. As a result, their name translates as "good mother."

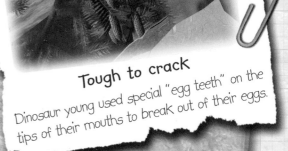

Tough to crack

Dinosaur young used special "egg teeth" on the tips of their mouths to break out of their eggs.

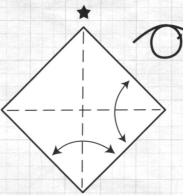

Make a Dinosaur Hatchling

Try out this simple-to-follow model of a hatchling.

★ ★

1 Start with the model sheet white side up. Valley fold along both diagonals, crease, and unfold.

2 Turn the paper over. Valley fold the edges together, crease, and unfold.

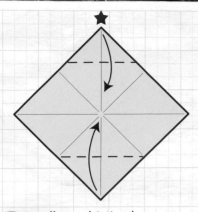

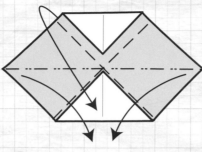

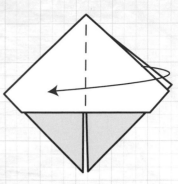

3 Valley fold the lower corner up to the center. Valley fold the upper corner down to just short of the center.

4 Using the creases made in steps 1 and 2, pull the top edge down and reverse fold the two outside points.

5 Your model should now look like this. Valley fold the top flap on the right over to the left.

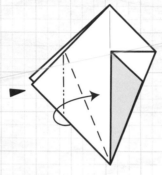

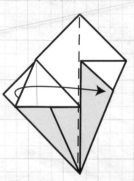

6 Valley fold the lower right edge to the center.

7 Fold the lower-left edge to the center, but open and flatten the point on the left (see the next diagram for guidance).

8 Now valley fold the top left-hand flap to the right.

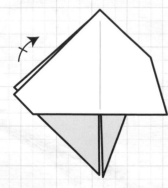

9 This is the result. Repeat steps 5 to 8 on the left-hand side.

FACT

Dinosaur eggs have been found in clutches of over 20 to a nest.

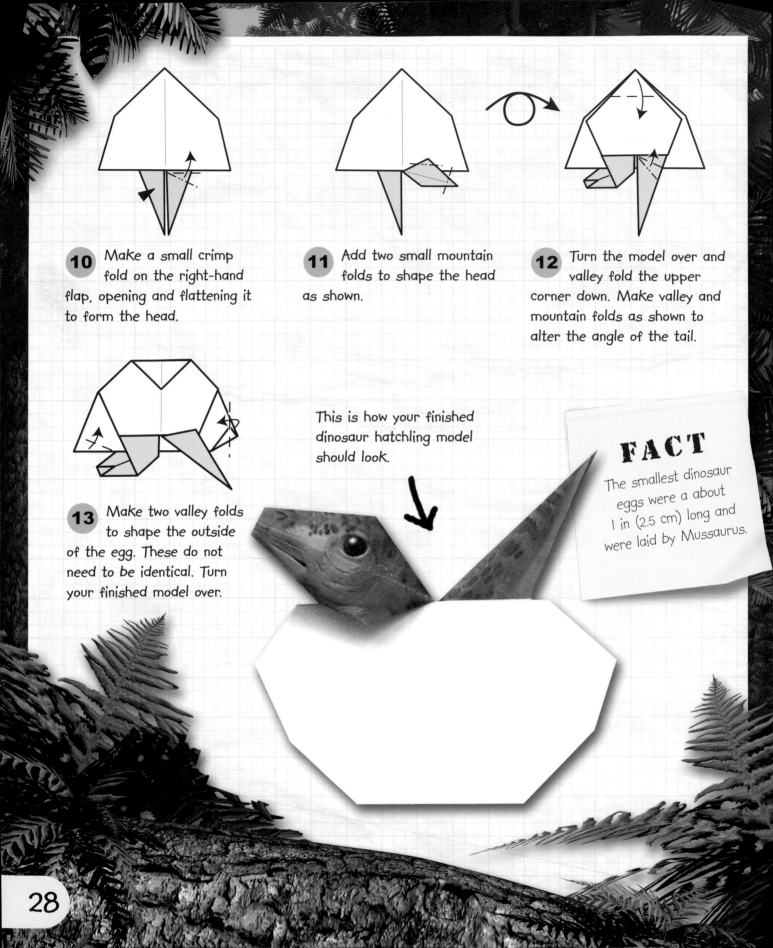

10 Make a small crimp fold on the right-hand flap, opening and flattening it to form the head.

11 Add two small mountain folds to shape the head as shown.

12 Turn the model over and valley fold the upper corner down. Make valley and mountain folds as shown to alter the angle of the tail.

13 Make two valley folds to shape the outside of the egg. These do not need to be identical. Turn your finished model over.

This is how your finished dinosaur hatchling model should look.

FACT

The smallest dinosaur eggs were a about 1 in (2.5 cm) long and were laid by Mussaurus.

Velociraptor

This terrifying dinosaur was one of the most fearsome prehistoric predators. It had razor-sharp teeth, was highly intelligent, and hunted prey in large, well-organized packs. Its most deadly feature, however, was the sharp claw on each of its hind feet. This was used as a lethal precision weapon—the velociraptor would grab hold of its prey and use the claw to slash through an artery or the windpipe and bring about a swift death.

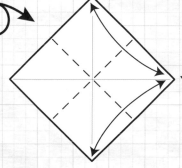

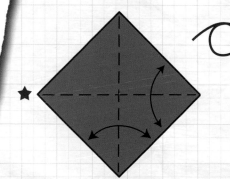

Balancing act

Velociraptors used their tails for balance while running—just like a cheetah does today.

Make a Velociraptor

DIFFICULTY ★★★☆

Practice your reverse folds before starting this model.

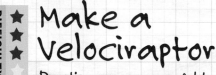

1 Start with the model sheet colored side up. Valley fold both diagonals, crease, and unfold.

2 Turn the paper over. Valley fold the edges together, crease, and unfold.

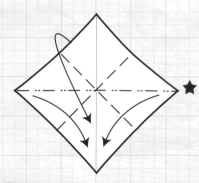

3 Using the creases already formed, fold the outer corners down to the bottom corner and flatten the upper quarter on top.

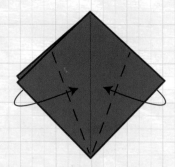

4 Valley fold the lower edges of the top layer in to the vertical center.

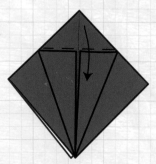

5 Valley fold the upper triangular flap down.

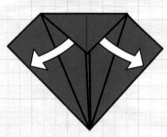

6 Unfold the flaps from under the triangular flap.

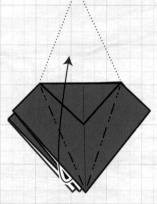

7 Unfold the top layer upward.

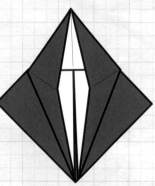

8 As the layer unfolds, push the outside corners into the center and flatten them to form a diamond.

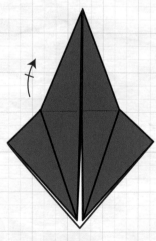

9 Turn the model over and repeat steps 4 to 8 on the other side.

FACT

Recently discovered evidence suggests that Velociraptors may have had a feathery covering on their arms and bodies.

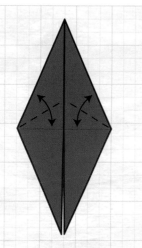

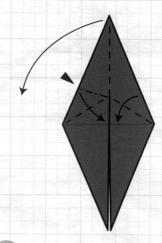

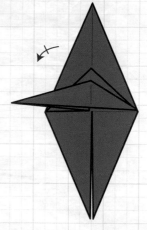

10 Valley fold both upper edges down to the horizontal crease, but crease only as far as the center.

11 Using the creases made in step 10, push the left-hand edge into the center and swing the leg section to the left, as shown, folding it in half as it moves down.

12 Repeat steps 10 and 11 on the reverse side, but fold the leg to the right so that both points meet.

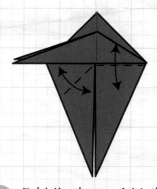

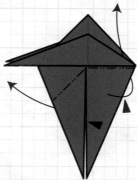

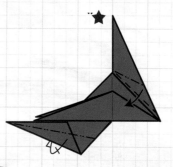

13 Fold the lower right flap upward as shown, crease, and unfold. Fold the lower-left flap over as shown, crease, and unfold.

14 Inside reverse fold both flaps using the creases made in step 13.

15 Narrow the left-hand flap with a mountain fold on both sides. Reposition the neck with valley and mountain folds.

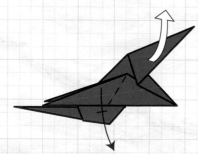

16 Valley fold the leg flaps on both sides downward and unfold the neck section.

17 Make a crimp fold on the neck, making sure that the two sides tuck inside the body.

18 Shape the arms with pleats. Make an inside reverse fold to start the head.

19 Valley fold both flaps down on either side of the head.

20 Inside reverse fold the tip of the head.

FACT
Velociraptor's sharp claw measured from 4 to 5 in (10 to 12 cm) long.

This is how your finished Velociraptor model should look.

Diplodocus

One of the largest land dinosaurs to have lived, Diplodocus grew to a length of nearly 100 ft (30 m) due mainly to its long neck and tail. It fed off cones and leaves from trees and may have stood on its rear legs, using its tail as an extra "leg" to reach the topmost branches. Because of its huge size, adult Diplodocus' were protected from attack by large meat eaters.

Cracking the whip
Diplodocus would have defended itself by thrashing its long tail like a whip.

FACT

Diplodocus lived during the Late Jurassic period, approximately 150 million years ago.

Make a Diplodocus

DIFFICULTY ★★★

Practice your inside reverse folds before starting this model.

1 Start with the model sheet white side up. Valley fold along a diagonal, crease, and unfold. Valley fold two outer corners to meet this crease.

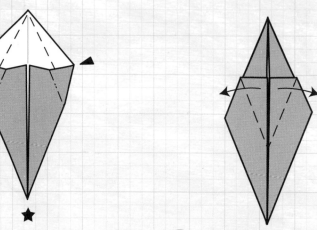

2 Fold the upper edges to the center, crease, and unfold.

3 Using the creases made in step 2, inside reverse fold the flaps.

4 Valley fold the top layers out as shown.

5 Valley fold the whole model in half from right to left.

6 Make two pleats where shown and crease them firmly.

FACT

Diplodocus translates as "double beam" and refers to the pair of flattened bones that grew beneath each tail bone. These stiffened the long, whiplike tail.

7 Unfold the pleats made in step 6.

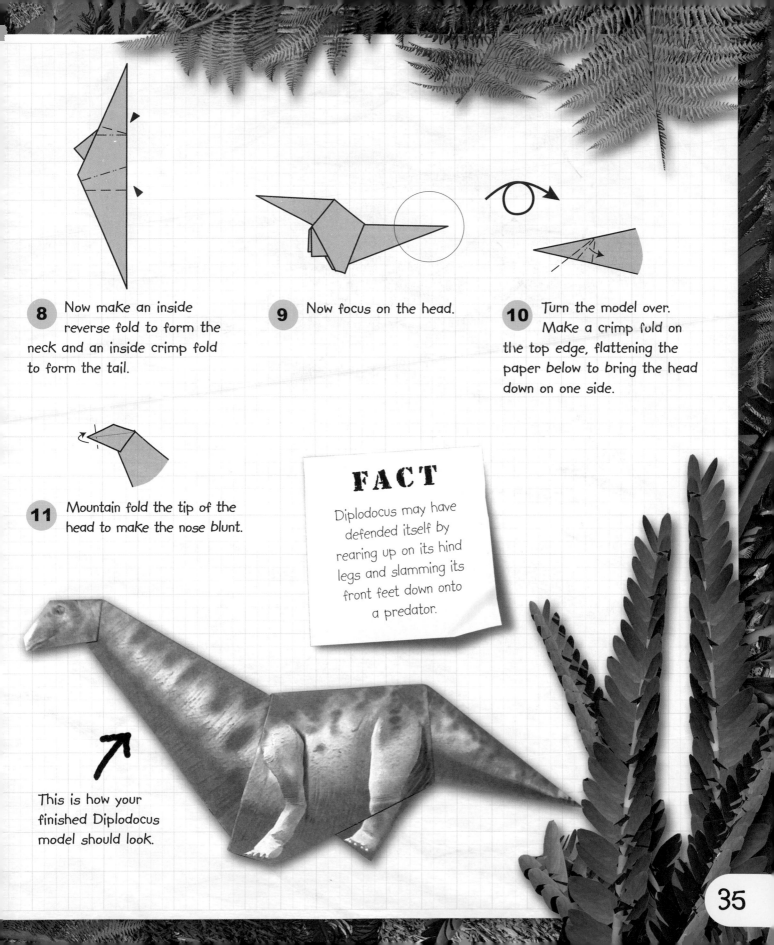

8 Now make an inside reverse fold to form the neck and an inside crimp fold to form the tail.

9 Now focus on the head.

10 Turn the model over. Make a crimp fold on the top edge, flattening the paper below to bring the head down on one side.

11 Mountain fold the tip of the head to make the nose blunt.

FACT

Diplodocus may have defended itself by rearing up on its hind legs and slamming its front feet down onto a predator.

This is how your finished Diplodocus model should look.

Pterosaur

Pterosaurs were a group of prehistoric reptiles that included Pteranodon. They were the first vertebrates (animals with backbones) to take to the air. They had thin sheets of skin, which were stretched between their finger bones and their ankles, that were used as wings. Pterosaurs first appeared during the Late Triassic period, some 190 million years ago, and evolved into a wide range of shapes and sizes.

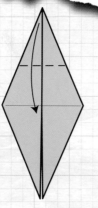

Stretched thin
The skin on a Pterosaur's wing may have been as little as 1/25 in (0.5 mm) thick!

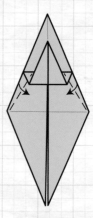

DIFFICULTY ★★★★

Make a Pterosaur
Fold your own terrifying Pterosaur!

1 Follow the first nine steps of the Velociraptor model. Valley fold the top corner down to a point just past halfway.

2 The Pterosaur's eyes should be visible on the lower layer. Leave a short gap and valley fold the top layer back up again.

3 Shape the sides of the top layer with valley folds.

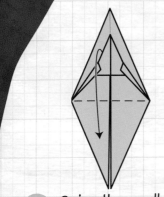

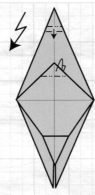

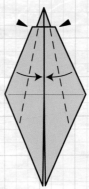

4 Swing the small, top flap downward.

5 Make a pleat fold in the beak of the Pterosaur and mountain fold the tip of the body underneath.

6 Turn the model over. Valley fold the top layer of each of the sides into the center, carefully squashing at the top.

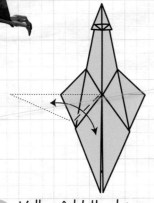

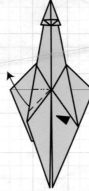

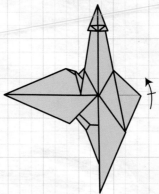

7 Valley fold the lower left-hand flap over so that the edge is horizontal. Crease and unfold.

8 Using the crease made in step 7, push the left-hand corner over to the left. As you push, flatten out the wing to form a diamond shape.

9 Your model should look like this. Repeat steps 7 and 8 on the right-hand side.

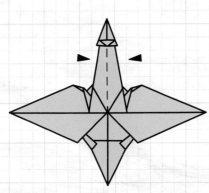

10 Squeeze the neck together to make it thinner. Turn over for the completed model.

This is how your finished Pterosaur model should look.

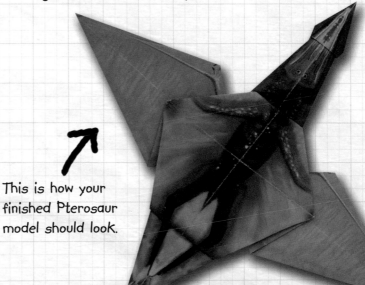

Plesiosaur

Plesiosaurs were perfectly adapted to life in the prehistoric oceans. They had powerful, streamlined bodies, flippers that were used to propel them through the water, and long, slender necks. These successful prehistoric creatures first appeared at the start of the Jurassic period, about 210 million years ago, and remained present in the Earth's oceans until the dinosaurs died out about 65 million years ago.

Gone fishing

The long neck of a Plesiosaur would dart out quickly to catch any swimming prey.

FACT

Plesiosaurs would have come ashore to lay eggs on a beach, just as turtles do today.

Make a Plesiosaur

DIFFICULTY ★★★★

Take care when folding the long neck on this model.

1. Start with the model sheet colored side up. Valley fold along a diagonal, crease, and unfold. Valley fold the outer corners in to the center.

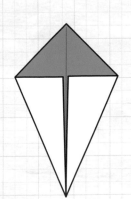

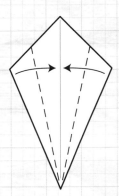

2 Turn the sheet over.

3 Valley fold both outer corners into the center.

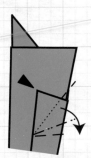

4 Make a pleat to form the tail.

5 Now valley fold the model in half down the center from left to right.

6 Valley fold the top layer in half to the right. Repeat on the other side.

7 Make the two creases shown on the uppermost layer. Using these creases, pull the corner down and flatten the layer. The dotted line shows where a new valley crease is formed on the second layer. Repeat on the other side.

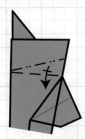

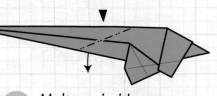

8 Make two creases in the rear section as shown. Using these creases, make an outside crimp fold to angle the back of the Plesiosaur.

9 Make a valley fold passing in a straight line to form the legs, crease, and unfold. Repeat on the other side.

10 Make an inside reverse fold on the neck. Remember to precrease the fold as a valley fold through all layers to make it easier.

11 Make another reverse fold at a slight angle to bring the head back up again.

12 Add a smaller reverse fold to form the head.

13 Valley fold each half of the head downward.

14 Add an inside reverse fold to the tip to blunt the nose.

15 Add mountain creases along either side of the neck to shape it. Fold out the legs halfway.

This is how your finished Plesiosaur model should look.

FACT

Elasmosaurus, a type of Plesiosaur, had a very long neck that contained 28 neck bones—even a long-necked giraffe only has seven!

Ophthalmosaurus

This dolphin-shaped prehistoric reptile swam through the Earth's seas about 145 million years ago. Its streamlined body could push through the water at speeds of up to 25 mph (40 km/h), hunting fish and squid to eat. It was also equipped with a very large pair of eyes—each about the same size as a dinner plate. These helped Opthalmosaurus to see deep beneath the surface and hunt where the light was very poor.

FACT

Even though it looked like a fish, Ophthalmosaurus needed to breath air, just like all other reptiles. It would have had to surface regularly to do so.

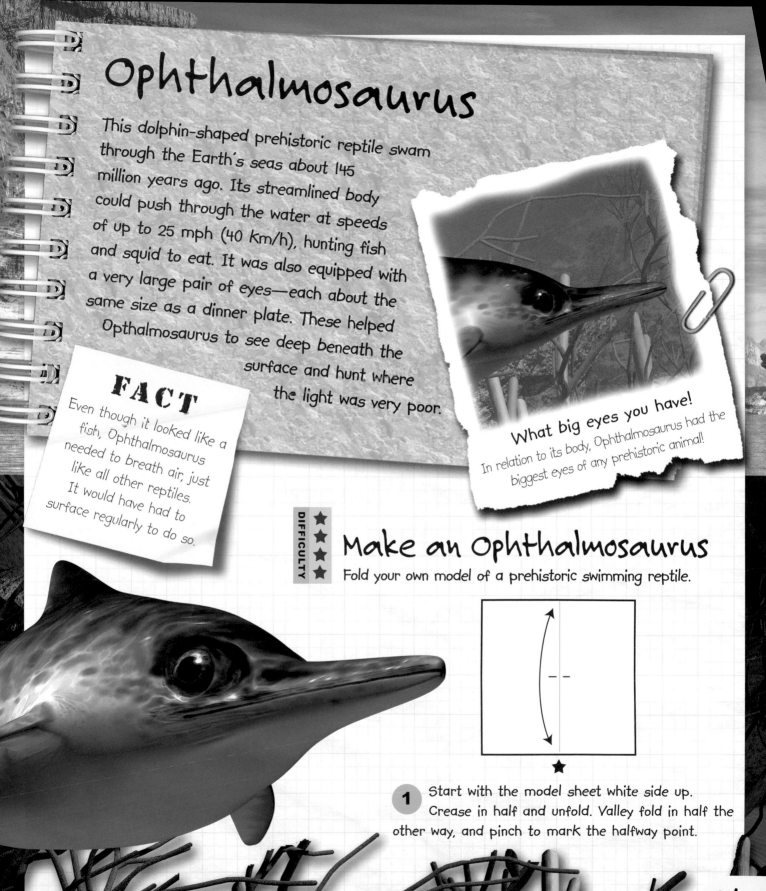

What big eyes you have!
In relation to its body, Ophthalmosaurus had the biggest eyes of any prehistoric animal!

DIFFICULTY ★★★★

Make an Ophthalmosaurus
Fold your own model of a prehistoric swimming reptile.

★

1 Start with the model sheet white side up. Crease in half and unfold. Valley fold in half the other way, and pinch to mark the halfway point.

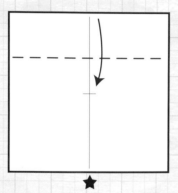

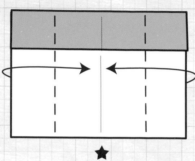

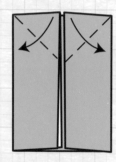

2 Valley fold the top edge down to meet the pinch.

3 Valley fold the sides in to the vertical center.

4 Valley fold the upper edges to meet the outside edges.

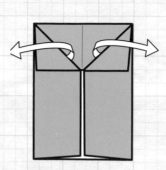

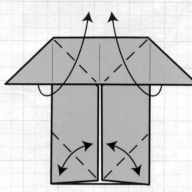

5 Carefully ease out a layer of paper on either side and flatten the long sections over the top.

6 Valley fold each half of the lower edge to the vertical center, crease, and unfold. Swing the top flaps up as shown.

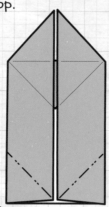

7 Inside reverse fold the lower corners.

FACT

Ophthalmosaurus belongs to a group of prehistoric animals called the Ichthyosaurs, which translates as "fish lizards."

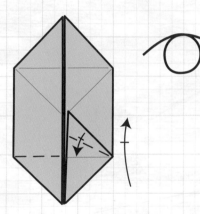

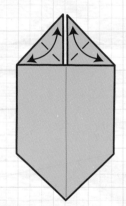

8 Valley fold the lower-right triangular flap up. Valley fold this triangular flap in half. Repeat on the other flap.

9 Turn the model over. Valley fold the triangular flap at the top in half, crease, and unfold.

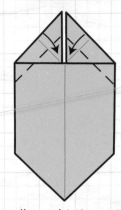

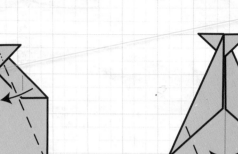

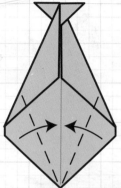

10 Valley fold the outer edges down to the point where the triangular flaps meet. This forms the tail. The tail flaps cross over each other.

11 This is the result. Valley fold the upper edges to the center. Crease firmly at the tail end.

12 Valley fold both lower edges in to the center.

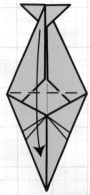

13 Valley fold the tail down, between the widest corners.

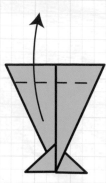

14 Leave a small gap, then valley fold the tail up again.

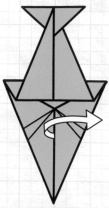

15 Peel open the flap on the lower-right edge.

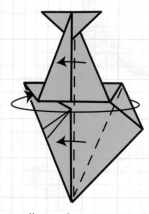

16 Valley fold the model in half, tucking the flap into the pocket behind the model's fin.

This is how your finished Ophthalmosaurus model should look.

Antarctosaurus

This monster-sized dinosaur belonged to the group of prehistoric reptiles called the Sauropods and was a distant relative of the Diplodocus. Measuring up to 130 ft (40 m) long, it may have been even larger than Diplodocus. Antarctosaurus roamed the planet during the Late Cretaceous period, about 70 million years ago, and was one of the last dinosaurs to appear.

Heavy meal
Sauropods like Antarctosaurus are known to have swallowed stones that ground up plant matter in their stomachs, making it easier to digest.

Make an Antarctosaurus

DIFFICULTY ★★★★

Follow these simple steps to create your own Antarctosaurus model.

★

1 Start with the model sheet white side up. Valley fold the edges together, crease, and unfold.

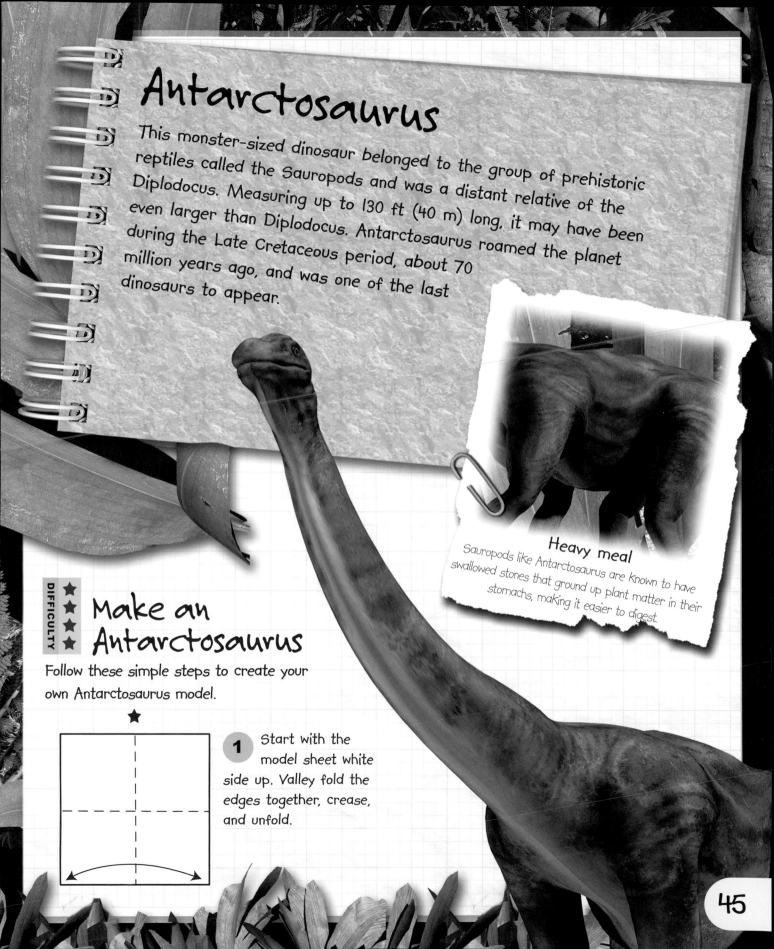

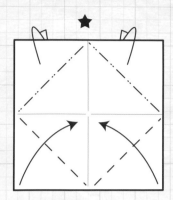

2 Valley fold the two lower corners to the center, and mountain fold the two upper corners to the center on the other side.

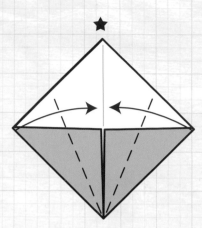

3 Valley fold the two lower edges to the center.

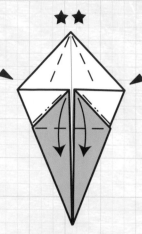

4 Valley fold the points folded in step 3 down, at the same time folding the upper edges to the center and flattening the outer points.

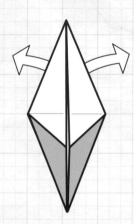

5 This is how your model should look. Unfold the two flaps from behind.

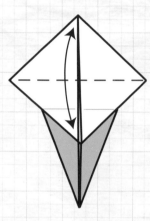

6 Valley fold the white square along a diagonal. Crease and unfold.

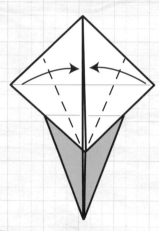

7 Valley fold the lower edges of the white square to the vertical center, as you did in step 3.

FACT

The name Antarctosaurus means "southern lizard." It came from South America.

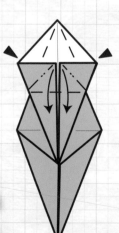

8 Repeat step 4 on the upper kite shape.

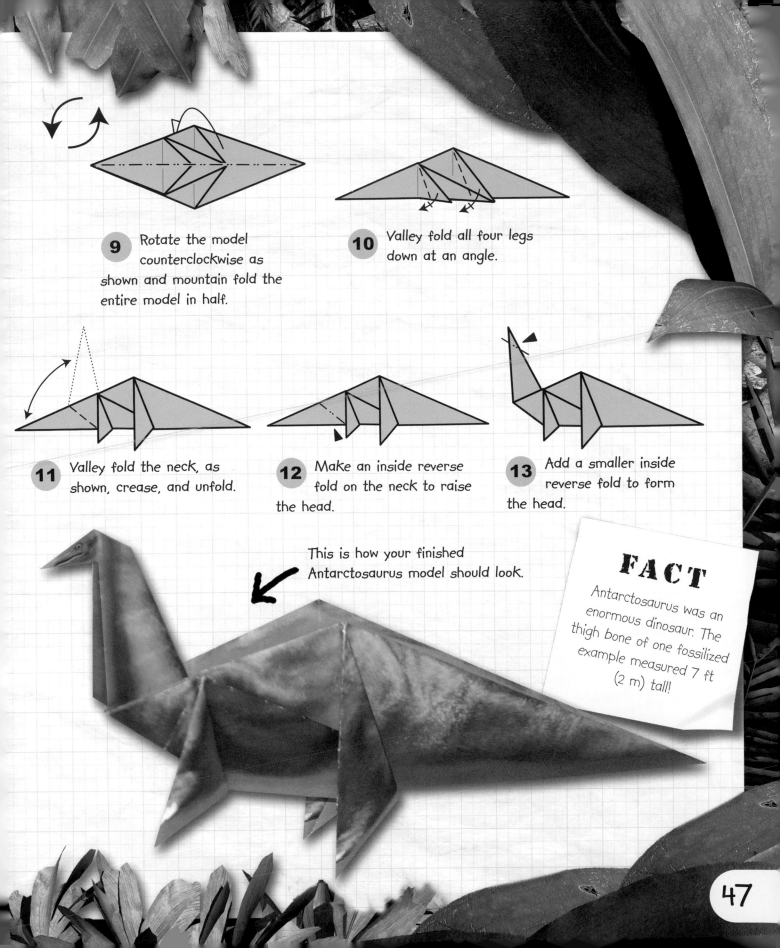

9 Rotate the model counterclockwise as shown and mountain fold the entire model in half.

10 Valley fold all four legs down at an angle.

11 Valley fold the neck, as shown, crease, and unfold.

12 Make an inside reverse fold on the neck to raise the head.

13 Add a smaller inside reverse fold to form the head.

This is how your finished Antarctosaurus model should look.

FACT

Antarctosaurus was an enormous dinosaur. The thigh bone of one fossilized example measured 7 ft (2 m) tall!

Tips and Tricks

Folding tip

Always work on a clear, flat surface and press your folds firmly with a clean finger. Fold slowly and do not crease until you are sure the paper is lined up properly.

Using the step-by-steps

If you find a step difficult, try looking ahead to the next diagram to see what your model should look like. Always read the words as well as looking at the diagram, but if you still have problems, leave the model for a while and go back to it. Make sure the paper matches the position shown in each step.

Using different paper

Experiment with different types of paper. Try with both thinner and thicker paper or gift wrap for a different look. Living subjects often look better when folded with paper that has some kind of texture.

Start with a square

Most origami models start as a square sheet of paper. If you are using paper from around the house, make sure that each side of the paper is exactly the same length, and cut it out carefully.

Origami Master

Once you have completed all of the amazing models in this book, you will be an origami master! But why stop there? On the Internet, there are many web sites with different models for you to try.

Tyrannosaurus Rex

Use with instructions on pages 6–7

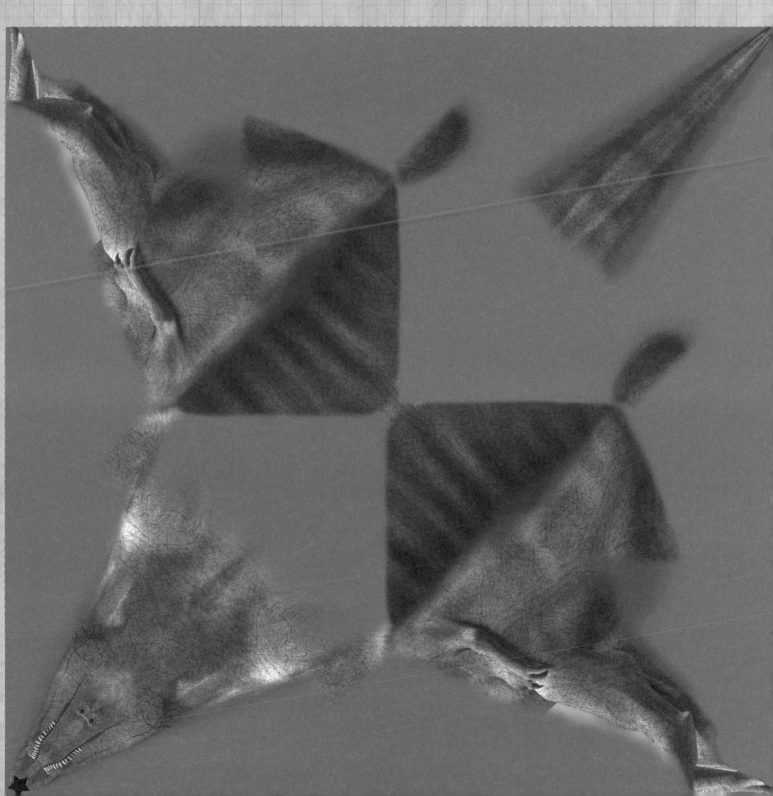

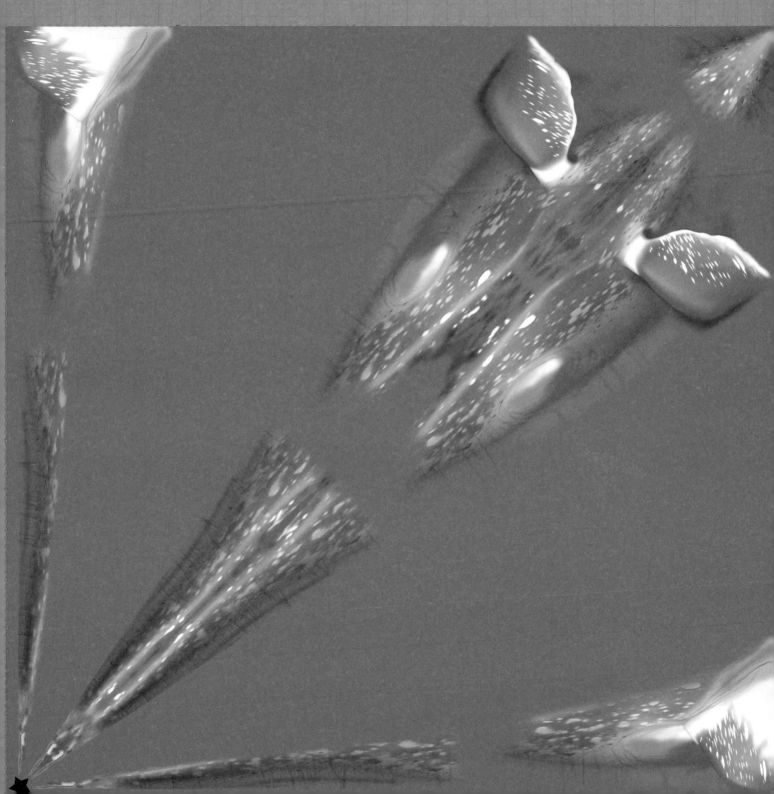

Ophthalmosaurus

Use with instructions on pages 41–44

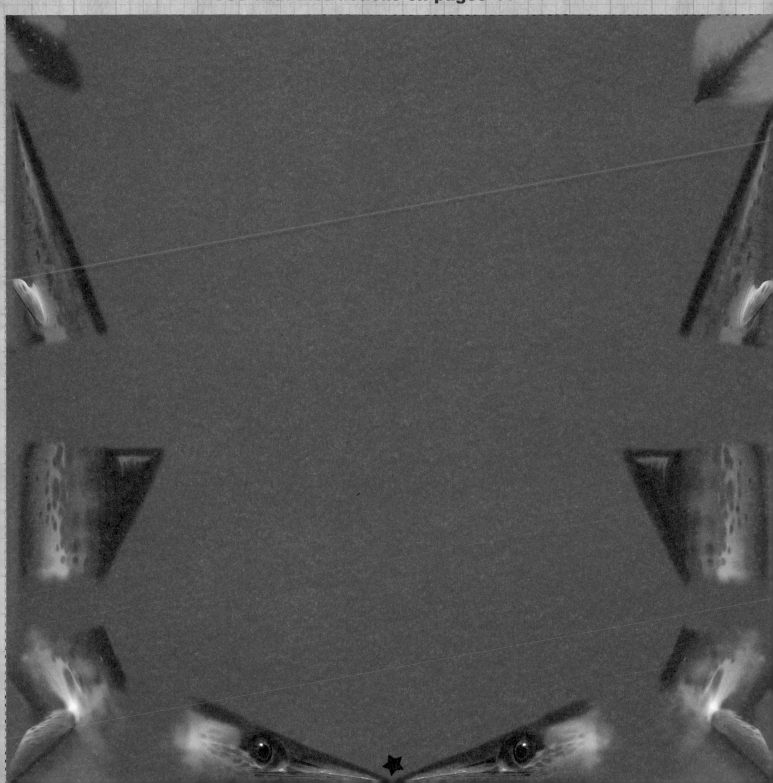

Antarctosaurus

Use with instructions on pages 45–47

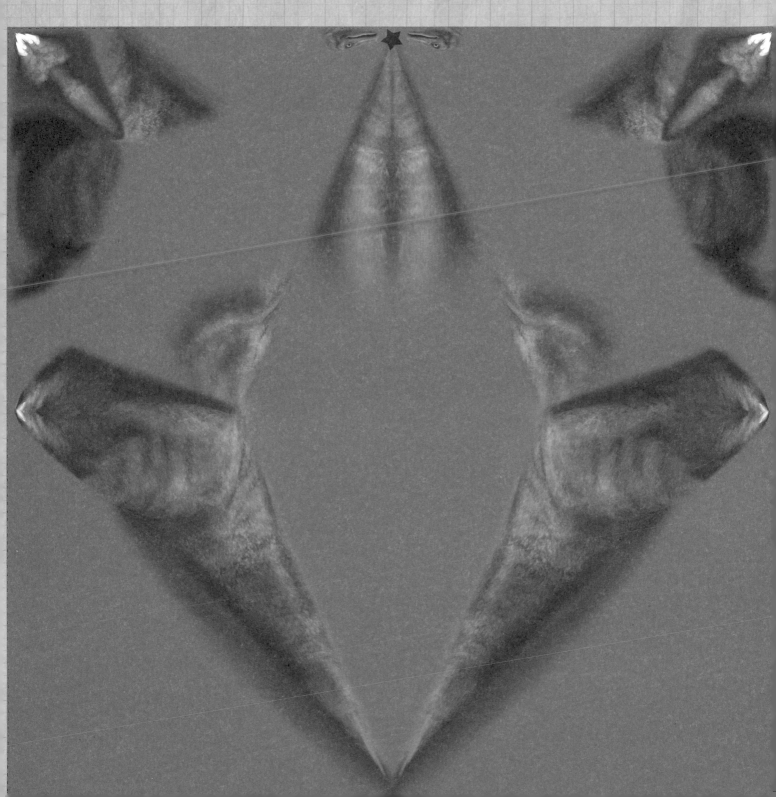

Dimetrodon

Use with instructions on pages 8–9

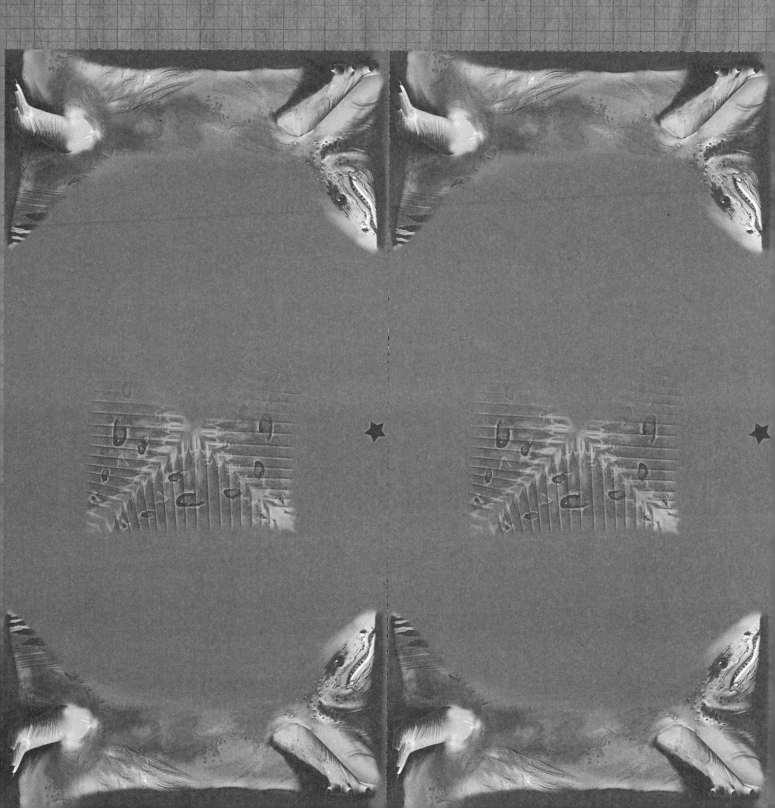

Pteranodon

Use with instructions on pages 10–11

Velociraptor

Use with instructions on pages 29–32

Pterosaur

Use with instructions on pages 36–37

Plesiosaur

Use with instructions on pages 38–40

Antarctosaurus

Use with instructions on pages 45–47

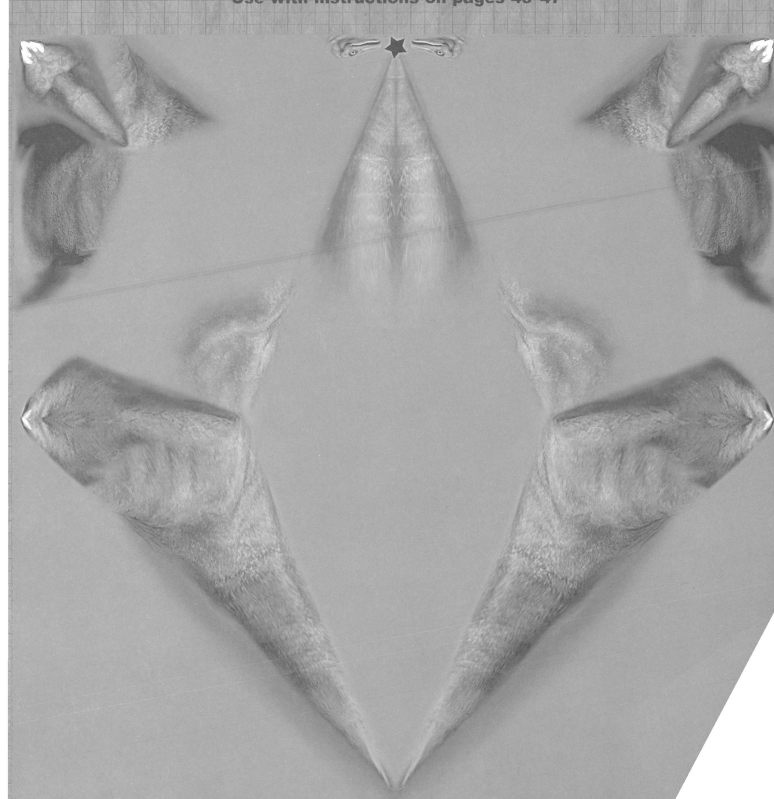